LIGHTHOUSES OF MICHIGAN

Help Us Keep This Guide Up to Date

Every effort has been made by the authors and editors to make this guide as accurate and useful as possible. However, many things can change after a guide is published—phone numbers change, facilities come under new management, etc.

We would love to hear from you concerning your experiences with this guide and how you feel it could be improved and be kept up to date. While we may not be able to respond to all comments and suggestions, we'll take them to heart and we'll also make certain to share them with the authors. Please send your comments and suggestions to the following address:

The Globe Pequot Press
Reader Response/Editorial Department
P. O. Box 480
Guilford, CT 06437

Or you may e-mail us at:

editorial@GlobePequot.com

Thanks for your input, and happy travels!

LIGHTHOUSES SERIES

LIGHTHOUSES OF MICHIGAN

A Guidebook and Keepsake

Bruce Roberts and Ray Jones

INSIDERS' GUIDE®

GUILFORD, CONNECTICUT
AN IMPRINT OF THE GLOBE PEQUOT PRESS

INSIDERS' GUIDE®

Copyright © 2005 by Bruce Roberts and Ray Jones

Text design by Schwartzman Design, Deep River, CT
Map design and terrain by Stephen C. Stringall, Cartography by M.A. Dubé
Map © The Globe Pequot Press
All photographs, unless otherwise credited, are by Bruce Roberts.

Library of Congress Cataloging-in-Publication Data
Roberts, Bruce, 1930-
    Lighthouses of Michigan : a guidebook and keepsake / Bruce Roberts and Ray Jones.
  —1st ed.
        p. cm. — (Lighthouses series)
    ISBN 0-7627-3738-7
    1. Lighthouses—Michigan—Guidebooks. I. Jones, Ray, 1948- II. Title. III. Lighthouses series (Globe Pequot Press)

    VK1024.M5R63 2005
    387.1'55'09774—dc22

                                                    2004060819

Manufactured in China
First Edition/Second Printing

The information listed in this guide was confirmed at press time. The ownership of many lighthouses, however, is gradually being transferred from the Coast Guard to private concerns. Please confirm visitor information before traveling.

DEDICATION

For Louis Bauchan, keeper of Michigan lighthouses for the U.S. Lighthouse Service for many years.

For my grandson, Ani Roberts

ACKNOWLEDGMENTS

Thanks to Bob and Sandra Shanklin, "The Lighthouse People," and to Rick Polad for their contributions of wonderful photography to this book.

CONTENTS

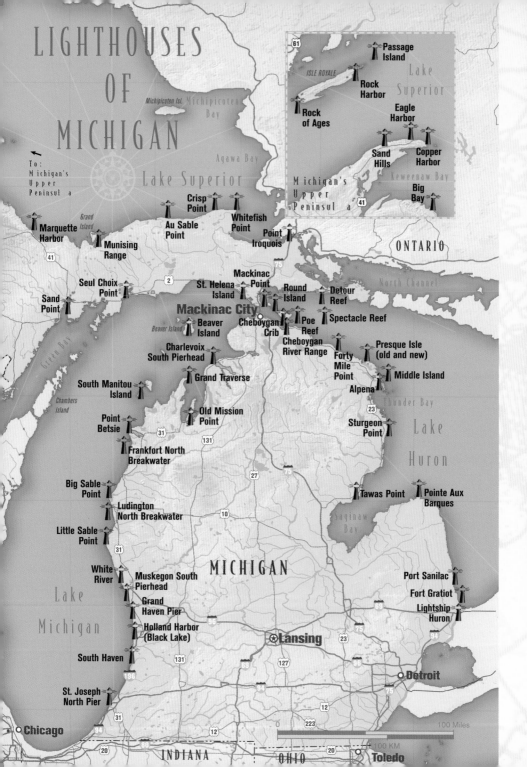

LIGHTHOUSES OF MICHIGAN

To: Michigan's Upper Peninsula

Lake Superior

Michipicoten Isl. Michipicoten Bay

Agawa Bay

Michigan's Upper Peninsula

Lake Superior

Isle Royale

Passage Island

Rock Harbor

Rock of Ages

Eagle Harbor

Sand Hills

Copper Harbor

Big Bay

Keweenaw Bay

Crisp Point

Au Sable Point

Whitefish Point

Point Iroquois

Marquette Harbor

Grand Island

Munising Range

ONTARIO

Seul Choix Point

Sand Point

St. Helena Island

Mackinac Point

Round Island

Detour Reef

North Channel

Mackinac City

Beaver Island

Cheboygan Crib

Poe Reef

Spectacle Reef

Beaver Island

Cheboygan River Range

Charlevoix South Pierhead

Presque Isle (old and new)

Forty Mile Point

Middle Island

Grand Traverse

South Manitou Island

Green Bay

Chambers Island

Alpena

Thunder Bay

Point Betsie

Old Mission Point

Sturgeon Point

Lake Huron

Frankfort North Breakwater

Big Sable Point

Ludington North Breakwater

Tawas Point

Pointe Aux Barques

Saginaw Bay

Little Sable Point

MICHIGAN

White River

Muskegon South Pierhead

Port Sanilac

Fort Gratiot

Lightship Huron

Lake Michigan

Grand Haven Pier

Holland Harbor (Black Lake)

Lansing

South Haven

St. Joseph North Pier

Detroit

Chicago

INDIANA

OHIO

Toledo

100 Miles

100 KM

INTRODUCTION

Although located hundreds of miles from the nearest salt water, closer to the heart of the North American continent than to the open ocean, Michigan is prime lighthouse country. With more than 3,000 miles of rugged shoreline to guard, nearly four times as much as California, Michigan can boast more lighthouses than any other state or Canadian province. Together, the Upper and Lower Peninsulas are home to more than one hundred historic navigational towers. In comparison, Maine has about sixty lighthouses, Florida about forty, and North Carolina only a dozen or so.

Michigan is probably more widely known for football, forests, fall color, fruit orchards, and, of course, automobiles than for lighthouses, but while it may come as a surprise to many, this solidly Midwestern state has a rich maritime tradition almost as old as America itself. Michigan is all but surrounded by water, and it has been that way since the end of the last ice age some 10,000 to 15,000 years ago. When the mountains of ice melted, they left behind five huge lakes, the largest bodies of freshwater on the planet, and today, four of these Great Lakes—Erie, Huron, Michigan, and Superior—touch the shores of Michigan.

Guiding Lights on an Inland Sea

The Great Lakes are *great* in every sense of the word. Covering 94,680 square miles of the continental interior in a cold blue blanket, they comprise some 5,475 cubic miles of freshwater in all. It would take more than fifty years for that much water to move down the Mississippi River into the Gulf of Mexico and centuries for it to pour through the narrow St. Lawrence and out into the Atlantic.

In essence the Great Lakes are a freshwater inland sea, and like other seas, they are fraught with danger for mariners. To navigate them safely, it is essential to know precisely where you are and where you are headed. The Ojibwa and other Native American mariners who braved these turbulent waters often turned their eyes to the sky for guidance. But while the sailor's friend, Polaris, can point the way north, it cannot warn of a dangerous shoal, help navigate a narrow, rock-strewn channel, or mark the passage to a safe harbor. For these purposes, sailors have long looked to certain man-made "stars" along the shore.

Great Lakes freighters carry an endless variety of raw materials and finished products—iron ore to steel mills, metal parts to auto assembly plants, oil and chemicals to refineries, and grain from the prodigious farms of the Midwest to hungry people all over the world. Much of this maritime commerce occurs along the Michigan shore, to or from Detroit, Saginaw, Ludington, Marquette, and other bustling ports.

The Great Lakes have been a driving force in the American economy. Long lake freighters, together with their brave crews, have fueled that engine. But this prosperity has come at a high price: thousands of ships sunk and many more thousands of sailors drowned or frozen to death in the lakes' dark and frigid waters.

The cost in vessels and lives would have been much higher if not for the sparkling constellation of lighthouses that ring each of the Great Lakes. About half of these sentinels are located in Michigan or just off the Michigan shore. Many of these lights, such as the one at Whitefish Point, have shone out over the lakes since America itself was young. Most are at least a century old, and some much older. All have played a vital role in the economic development and history of the Midwest and the United States as a whole.

The Saga of the *Edmund Fitzgerald*

No doubt, Michigan's lighthouses have saved countless ships and lives, but fate has placed more than a few beyond saving. Among the legendary shipwrecks of the Great Lakes, none is more widely known and celebrated than that of the *Edmund Fitzgerald*. The magnificent ore freighter and its crew of twenty-nine men met a tragic and mysterious end on November 10, 1975.

When the *Edmund Fitzgerald* launched at River Rouge, Michigan, on a bright June day in 1958, she was the world's largest freshwater freighter. Named for a successful Milwaukee banker, she was as proud a ship as was ever lapped by lake water. Her long, clean lines made her a fond and familiar sight to residents of port cities and towns from Toledo to Duluth. She became such a star that a Detroit newspaper ran a regular column to keep readers informed of her activities.

Indeed, the *Big Fitz*—the affectionate nickname used by her crew—was quite a ship. Able to carry more than 25,000 tons of iron ore, she had a muscular, 7,000-horsepower steam turbine that could whisk the big ship and her enormous cargo along at better than 16 miles per hour. From 1958 onward, year after year, she set one record after another for carrying bulk freight. Usually the records she broke were her own. By the time the *Edmund Fitzgerald* steamed out of Duluth on the afternoon of Sunday, November 9, 1975, she had plied the shipping channels of the Great Lakes for more than seventeen years. She was still in her prime, by lake standards, and just as solid and capable as the day she was launched.

On this trip her holds were filled to the brim with 26,013 tons of taconite, marble-size pellets of milled iron ore. Often she carried passengers as well as cargo and had two luxury staterooms and a comfortable lounge to accommodate them. But the Great Lakes are notorious for the dark, howling storms that churn their waters in November. Potential lake passengers are wary of the month and choose to travel shipboard earlier in the year. So the *Fitzgerald* left Duluth carrying only the taconite and twenty-nine lake sailors.

Most members of the crew were Midwesterners; fourteen of them were from Ohio and eight from Wisconsin. A few came from as far away as Florida and California. All were seasoned sailors, and older members of the crew especially had weathered many a raging Lake Superior gale. The men ranged from their mid-twenties to near retirement age. At sixty-two, Captain Ernest McSorley was among the oldest.

According to McSorley's friends, the *Big Fitz* was, after his wife and family in Toledo, the love of his life. He knew the freighter's every quirk and idiosyncrasy— her tendency to roll queasily or to bend and spring like a rebounding diving board in high waves. But McSorley had resolute faith in the ability of the *Fitzgerald* to weather a storm—even a Lake Superior storm in November. Perhaps that is why, when Monday, November 10, dawned, bringing gale warnings and fierce winds, McSorley kept the *Fitzgerald*'s bow pointed down the lake toward Whitefish Point and Sault Ste. Marie.

Like a great, watery bull-dozer, Lake Superior is reshaping the sandy shores of the Upper Michigan Peninsula. Preservationists have struggled to hold back the lake and prevent it from claiming the historic Crisp Point tower.

The Big Bay Lighthouse is now a bed-and-breakfast inn, but its light remains active and still guides mariners.

The *Arthur M. Anderson*, a U.S. Steel ore carrier under the command of Captain J. B. Cooper, had left Duluth not long after the *Fitzgerald*. When the weather turned unexpectedly sour, McSorley made radio contact with Cooper, whose ship trailed his own by about 10 miles. The two captains agreed to stay in close communication and decided jointly that their ships would slip out of the traditional freighter channel along the lake's southern shores. Instead, they would steer for the northeast, where the leeward shore might provide some protection from the weather. They would soon discover, however, that there was no shelter from this storm. By midday on the 10th, the *Fitzgerald* and *Anderson* were battling 70 mile per hour winds and 30-foot waves.

By the middle of the afternoon, the *Fitzgerald* had begun to show the beating she was taking. The force of the storm snapped the heavy cable fencing around the deck and washed it away. The ship took a more threatening blow when the waves smashed through a pair of ventilator covers. About 3:30 P.M. Captain McSorley radioed the *Anderson* to report that he had water coming in. His vessel was operating at a list. Would the *Anderson* try to close the distance between the two ships? Yes, she would, came the reply.

The blasting wind and spray and the cloak of darkness that the storm had thrown over the lake made the *Fitzgerald* invisible to the unassisted eye, but her enormous hull put a substantial blip on the *Anderson*'s radar screen. In the fury of this gale, however, even radar contact was tenuous. Occasionally, when the towering waves swelled up to block the signal, the blip representing the *Fitzgerald* would flicker and disappear from the screen.

Despite the damage, the *Fitzgerald* plowed steadily onward through the storm. Apparently, McSorley was making for Whitefish Bay, where he hoped to find calmer waters. If he could round Whitefish Point into the bay, he might get his *Big Fitz* out of harm's way.

A lighthouse has stood on strategic Whitefish Point since 1849. In all the years since, rare has been the night when sailors on the lake could not count on its powerful light for guidance. But November 10, 1975, was just such a night. The early winter storm that had whipped Lake Superior into such a pitching cauldron had also vented its rage on the shore. It ripped down road signs, uprooted trees, and even bowled over a heavily loaded tractor trailer on the Mackinac Bridge. Among the utility poles snapped by the high winds was one feeding electric power to the Whitefish Point Lighthouse. And so, ironically, on the night when the *Edmund Fitzgerald* needed it most, there was no light at Whitefish Point.

Captain McSorley put out a call to all ships in his vicinity. Could anyone see the light at Whitefish Point? He got an immediate reply from the Swedish freighter *Avafors* in Whitefish Bay. The pilot reported that neither the light nor the radio beacon at Whitefish Point was operating. The pilot inquired about conditions out on the lake.

"Big sea," said McSorley. "I've never seen anything like it in my life."

As the storm raged on into the evening, an officer on the *Anderson* radioed the *Fitzgerald*. "How are you making out?" he asked. "We are holding our own," came the reply. Those words were the last ever heard from the *Edmund Fitzgerald*.

The men on the bridge of the *Anderson* had grown used to the wavering, ghostly radar image of the *Fitzgerald*. The sea return (radar interference caused by high waves) in this storm was tremendous. First the ship was there, then gone, then back again. Then, at some point shortly after 7:00 P.M. (no one aboard the *Anderson* ever knew exactly when), the *Edmund Fitzgerald* disappeared from the screen. And she did not return.

Minutes passed. Officers on the *Anderson* bridge checked their radar equipment. There were other ships on the screen—upbound freighters struggling through the heavy weather. But there was no sign of the *Fitzgerald*. Cooper ordered his men to try to take a visual sighting, but where the ship's running lights should have been, there was only darkness. Frantic attempts to reach the *Fitzgerald* on radio were answered with silence.

Wasting no time, Captain Cooper called the Coast Guard. "No lights," he said. "Don't have her on radar. I know she's gone."

A massive search-and-rescue operation swung into action. Despite the savage weather, freshwater and saltwater freighters alike changed course and steamed toward the *Fitzgerald*'s last-known position. Equally prepared to face the dangers of the storm were coastguardsmen, who rushed their fast cutters out onto the lake to join the search. Squadrons of aircraft, including huge C-130 transports and helicopters equipped with powerful searchlights, crisscrossed the waters off Whitefish Point. But there was no sign of the *Fitzgerald*, nor of survivors. The Whitefish Point Lighthouse, which by now was back in operation, flung its light out over a Lake Superior seemingly empty of any trace of the *Edmund Fitzgerald*. Apparently, the lake had swallowed whole the ship, cargo, and crew.

The search went on for days, but to little effect. By the end of the week, all members of the ill-fated crew were officially pronounced dead. Family, close friends, and colleagues, who had already begun their grieving, gathered in homes and chapels in Toledo, Detroit, Duluth, and other towns and cities along the shores of the Great Lakes. Church bells rang twenty-nine times as the mourners paid tribute to memories of their friends, relatives, and lovers—but not to their earthly remains. None of the bodies was ever recovered.

What happened? What could cause a ship the size of the *Fitzgerald* to sink so suddenly and vanish so completely? After an official inquiry the Coast Guard pointed a collective finger of blame at the *Fitzgerald*'s hatch covers. If they were loose or had been damaged by the storm, the high waves washing over the deck would have poured through the hatches and flooded the cargo holds. Having lost critical buoyancy, the big ship would have plunged to the bottom. Another theory put forward by several of McSorley's fellow freighter captains suggests that, perhaps unknowingly, he had grazed a shoal off Caribou Island. The damage caused by striking the shoal may have led to the flooding that took down the *Fitzgerald*.

Probably the most popular theory concerning the wreck maintains that a pair of towering waves raised the bow and the stern of the ship simultaneously, leaving unsupported the long center section, with its heavy cargo of iron ore. This might have caused the ship to snap in two, with the stern section rapidly following the bow to the bottom. But of course no one will ever know for sure what killed the *Fitzgerald* or what took place during those crucial moments before she went down. There were no witnesses left alive to tell the tale.

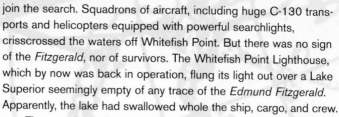

Which way is north? Both during the day and at night, lighthouses help mariners keep their bearings and find their way to safe harbor. This compass is in the Old Presque Isle Lighthouse.

Your Own Michigan Lighthouse Adventure

Michigan's lighthouses have many fascinating stories to tell, not all of them as tragic as that of the *Edmund Fitzgerald*. In *Lighthouses of Michigan*, you will read about the near miraculous construction of open-water towers near the Straits of Mackinac or on the Rock of Ages in Lake Superior. You'll learn about range lights, first designed and used on the Great Lakes, and skeleton towers like the one at Whitefish Point on the Upper Peninsula. And, of course, there are other shipwreck stories like that of the *Griffon*, the *Carl D. Bradley*, and the dozens of large vessels lost during the hurricane-like blizzard of 1913. Read the stories, learn the facts, and then stake your claim to a share of America's treasured maritime heritage by going out to visit a Michigan lighthouse.

Every corner of the Michigan coast has at least one historic lighthouse, and many stand within easy driving distance from large cities and towns such as Detroit, Saginaw, Grand Rapids, Marquette, and Houghton. This book takes you to most of the accessible Michigan lighthouses and to some that simply can't be reached.

As you'll see, the book is divided into three sections: Lights along Lake Huron, Lights along Lake Michigan, and Lights along Lake Superior. Within the sections lighthouses are presented geographically. This arrangement should make it easier to plan your own Michigan light-house outings—so should the directions, telephone contacts, and other travel information included at the end of each listing.

Generally, you should be able to visit the most attractive light-houses in one or another of the sections mentioned above in one or two long weekend excursions. To help you select the lighthouses you want to visit, individual listings include advice in the form of simple symbols: ▣ for lighthouses that are especially historic, 🚗 for lighthouses that are accessible by car, by boat, or on foot, 🤚 for visitor-friendly lighthouses that are frequently open to the public and feature museums or similar attractions, and 📷 for lighthouses that are particularly photogenic. For added convenience, every listing includes an easy-to-read summary of key information on the light-house: location, date the light was established, current status, height of the tower, type of optic, range, characteristic, and elevation of the beacon, and for all active lighthouses, the precise latitude and longi-tude of the beacon.

We hope you enjoy your Michigan lighthouse adventure.

CHAPTER ONE:
LIGHTS ALONG LAKE HURON

The Great Lakes are no ordinary bodies of freshwater. They are enormous inland seas hundreds of miles in length. Even more than saltwater sailors, mariners here need lighthouses to guide them, especially where low headlands offer few distinctive features. "It's like trying to navigate in a wheat field," said one frustrated sea captain after he brought his oceangoing freighter down the length of the St. Lawrence Seaway. But the Great Lakes lighthouses serve an even more important function: They save lives. On the wind-torn waters of these lakes, safety is always the first consideration, and sailors keep a close eye on the weather. In a storm, lighthouses provide mariners with a comforting visual anchor.

Lake sailors know the Midwest's worst storms come in the late fall. November brings a marrow-deep chill to the bones of sailors on the Great Lakes. It's not just that the weather gets colder, it's also that the lakes themselves take on a different character. They turn tempestuous and develop sharp, unpredictable tempers. Storms can blacken their faces in a matter of minutes and churn their waters into a confusion of towering waves capable of breaking a ship in half.

When old lake sailors gather to tell stories of the calamities brought on by the year's eleventh month, there is one November they rarely leave out, that is, the November of 1913. Those who were superstitious about numbers said it would be an unlucky year; but up until the fall, 1913 had proved them wrong. The spring and summer had been kind to the Great Lakes, providing sailors with a seemingly endless string of warm, clear days and calm, starry nights. Business was booming, and the large and growing fleet of freighters operating on the lakes set records for shipping.

Then came October and, with it, high winds howling out of the west. A record cold snap sent temperatures plunging below zero, and a series of early snowstorms dusted the lakes' shores with white. But for all its chill and bluster, October's unexpected outburst did little damage—a broken rudder here, a severed anchor chain there, and a couple of old wooden steamers run aground.

The year's fourth and final quarter had gotten off to an ominous start, but with lucrative contracts in their hands, captains were not willing to tie up their vessels for the season. They were determined to make 1913 the best year ever for shipping on the Great Lakes. But it was not to be.

At first, November seemed likely to reverse the unsettling trend of the previous month. For a week gentle breezes rippled the lakes, and the temperatures were downright balmy. But experienced sailors knew these pleasant conditions would not hold for long, not at this time of year; how right they were. Even as they hung up their uniform jackets to enjoy the unseasonable temperatures in shirtsleeves while their freighters cut through glass-smooth water, three deadly weather systems were headed their way. One rushed in with freezing winds from the Bering Sea; another poured over the Rockies, carrying an immense load of water from as far off as the South Pacific; and a third came spinning up, cyclone style, from the Caribbean. The three slammed into one another over the Great Lakes on or about November 7, 1913, creating what was in effect an inland hurricane.

This extraordinary storm struck with little or no warning. Dozens of freighters were caught in midlake, far from safe anchorage or, worse, near ship-killing rocks, shoals, and shallows. High waves battered hulls, and freezing spray caked decks and wheelhouses in a thick layer of ice. Swirling snow squalls blinded captains, pilots, and navigators, while high winds drove their vessels ever closer to disaster. The storm raged on without pause for five long days. By the time the clouds broke and the winds died down, on November 12, more than forty ships had been wrecked. Down with them went 235 sailors and passengers. Only a few of the bodies were ever recovered.

When the storm first assaulted Huron on November 7, its shipping lanes were filled with vessels crossing northwestward toward Michigan and Superior or southeastward toward Erie. As darkness set in, lighthouse beacons called to these ships from many points along the Michigan shore. There were safe harbors in this storm, and the lights marked the way. But most ships could not reach them or make any headway at all against the fierce westerly winds. Many captains pointed their bows toward the northeast and made a run for the Canadian side, where they hoped to find some protection. Many never made it. Huron's mountainous waves chewed up dozens of ships, and the lake's deep waters swallowed them whole. At least eight large freighters—the *McGean*, *Carruthers*, *Hydrus*, *Wexford*, *Scott*, *Regina*, *Price*, and *Argus*—all disappeared from the lake without a trace. Vanishing with them were 178 passengers and crewmen.

LIGHTSHIP HURON

Commissioned in 1921 as *Lightship No. 103*, the vessel known today as the *Huron* was used as a relief ship for Lake Michigan's Twelfth Lighthouse District. The *103* would replace lightships temporarily out of service while under repair. After fourteen years of filling in for others, the *103* took over a station of its own at Gray's Reef, Michigan. Later it served at Manitou Shoals on northern Lake Michigan, then in 1935 at Corsica Shoals in Lake Huron. Here its beacon helped guide traffic in and out of the narrow dredged channel that allowed large vessels to navigate the St. Clair River and lower Lake Huron.

The 97-foot lightship came equipped with a 52.5-foot lantern mast and a 5,000-pound mushroom anchor. It originally was steam powered, but in 1949 it received a diesel engine, radar, and radio beacon.

The *Huron* was the last lightship to serve on the Great Lakes. When it was finally decommissioned in 1970, the city of Port Huron bought the ship. Two years later, *Lightship 103* began a new era of service, this time as a museum and National Historic Landmark.

TO SEE THE LIGHT: The lightship rests in Pine Grove Park in Port Huron. From Interstate 94, drive south onto Pine Grove Street (Highway 25), turn left onto Prospect Street, and follow it 1 block to the parking area. The lightship and museum are open daily Memorial Day through Labor Day. For more information call (810) 982–0891 or visit www.ph museum.org.

Location: Port Huron

Established: 1921

Tower height: 52 feet
(light mast)

Elevation of the focal
plane: 52 feet

Status: Decommissioned
1970

Note: Last lightship to
serve on the Great Lakes

FORT GRATIOT LIGHT

In addition to the *Huron*, the last lightship to serve the Great Lakes, Port Huron can boast Michigan's oldest light station. The Fort Gratiot Light Station dates from 1825, well before Michigan became a state in 1837. After almost one and three-quarters centuries of service, the station still marks the Lake Huron entrance to the St. Clair River.

The original tower did not last long. The materials and workmanship were so shoddy that the tower collapsed within four years. A new tower went up in 1829, this one more sturdily constructed, with thick, conical walls of stone overlaid with brick. It still stands and remains in operation. Automated in 1933, its 82-foot height gives the beacon a focal plane 82 feet above Lake Michigan. The white tower,

redbrick keeper's cottage, and fog-whistle house are an active Coast Guard facility and rarely open to the public. In deference to its historic significance, however, visitors are allowed on the grounds a few times a year so that they can view Michigan's oldest lighthouse up close and personal.

TO SEE THE LIGHT: From I–94 take Pine Grove Street (Highway 25) north. Turn right onto Garfield Street and follow it to Gratiot Avenue. Parking is available in the area. For tours call (810) 982–3659, or ask at the nearby Huron Lightship Museum (see description on page 10).

Location: Port Huron

Established: 1825

Tower height: 86 feet

Elevation of the focal plane: 82 feet

Optic: Aerobeacon

Status: Active

Characteristic: Flashes green every 6 seconds

Range: 18 miles

Position: 43° 00' 24
82° 25' 24

Note: Michigan's oldest light station

Bob and Sandra Shanklin,
The Lighthouse People

Location: Port Sanilac

Established: 1886

Tower height: 59 feet

Elevation of the focal
plane: 69 feet

Optic: Fresnel
(fourth-order)

Status: Active

Characteristic: Flashes 3
times every 10 seconds

Range: 16 miles

Position: 43° 25' 48
82° 32' 24

Note: Unusual stepped
architecture

Once a vital link in a 300-mile chain of navigational lights guiding vessels along Michigan's eastern shores, the Port Sanilac beacon was the first light mariners saw as they exited the St. Clair River and steamed northward into Lake Huron. Although its importance as a navigational aid has diminished with time, the light remains in operation. The fourth-order Fresnel lens atop the 59-foot octagonal tower remains in use. The station's unusual step-sided brick keeper's dwelling is now a private residence.

TO SEE THE LIGHT: Now a private home, the lighthouse is not open to the public. However, it can be viewed from the end of a breakwater off Cherry Street in Port Sanilac.

This lighthouse is located on a strategic headland near the spot where Saginaw Bay opens into Lake Huron. French traders called the place Pointe aux Barques, or Point of Little Boats, because of the many canoes that used to gather here during fur-trading season. A town grew up here and, after Michigan became part of the United States, grew into a prime shipping port.

In 1848 the federal government approved $5,000 to build a lighthouse at Pointe aux Barques. It proved far less than adequate, and nine years later, it was replaced by the 89-foot conical brick tower that still stands here. Originally fitted with a state-of-the-art third-order Fresnel lens, the station now employs an automated optic. Its powerful flashing white light is visible from 18 miles out on Lake Huron. The beautiful classic lens that once served here can now be seen at the Grice Museum in Port Austin.

TO SEE THE LIGHT: To reach the lighthouse, take Highway 25 to Lighthouse Road. The county park, where the lighthouse stands, is about 10 miles east of Port Austin and 6 miles north of Port Hope.

Location: Port Austin

Established: 1848

Tower height: 89 feet

Elevation of the focal plane: 93 feet

Optic: Aerobeacon

Status: Active

Characteristic: Flashes twice every 20 seconds

Range: 28 miles

Position: 44° 01' 24 82° 47' 36

Note: Marks the lower lip of Saginaw Bay

The park offers camping and picnicking facilities. The lighthouse contains a pair of fascinating museums, one devoted to the lighthouse itself and the other to underwater archaeology. The museums and gift shop are open daily in summer, weekends only after Labor Day. Call (989) 428–4749 or go to www.pointeauxbarques lighthouse.org.

Just northwest of the lighthouse, the Huron City Museum showcases nineteenth-century life and times. Hours vary Memorial Day through September; closed the rest of the year. Take Highway 25 via Huron City Road. Call (989) 428–4123 or go to www.huroncity museums.org.

B uilt in 1853 to mark the northern entrance to Saginaw Bay, the first Tawas Point Lighthouse served for only twenty years. By the 1870s the rapidly shifting shoreline had placed the light more than a mile from the water, rendering it useless. The Lighthouse Board appealed to Congress for funds to build a new structure, and in 1876 a 68-foot tower, fitted with a rotating fourth-order Fresnel lens, began operating on a site closer to the bay. Its light can still be seen.

The lighthouse has an enclosed passageway intended to provide easy access to the tower, a feature no doubt appreciated by keepers here on the shores of blizzard-prone Lake Huron.

The Tawas Point Light sits on the grounds of Tawas Point State Park. Tours of the tower are available on summer weekends.

TO SEE THE LIGHT: Follow U.S. Highway 23 for about 1.5 miles west of Tawas City; then turn right onto Tawas Beach Road, which will take you to Tawas Point State Park. Drive to the beach parking area at the end of the road. Follow the walking path to the lighthouse. The tower is open to the public for tours on Saturday and Sunday from Memorial Day through Labor Day. Call (989) 362–5041.

Location: Tawas City

Established: 1853

Tower height: 68 feet

Elevation of the
focal plane: 70 feet

Optic: Fresnel
(fourth-order)

Status: Active

Characteristic: Occulting
(white with red sector)

Range: 16 miles

Position: 44° 15' 12
83° 26' 54

Note: Marks northern
approach to Saginaw Bay

STURGEON POINT LIGHT

Not far from Sturgeon Point on Lake Huron, a deadly reef lies in wait for unwary vessels. Built in 1870 to warn mariners to steer clear of this dangerous obstacle, the Sturgeon Point Light has prevented countless accidents. Even so, many vessels have wrecked practically in the shadow of its 68-foot tower. On the station grounds sits a big rudder salvaged from the wooden steamer *Marine City*, which burned near here in an 1880 disaster just off Sturgeon Point. Also lost nearby were the 233-ton schooner *Venus* in 1887, the three-masted schooner *Ispeming* in 1903, the *Clifton* in a 1924 gale, and many other vessels.

The Alcona County Historical Society owns the station, and the old keeper's residence houses museum exhibits. The light, automated since 1939, remains active. Occasionally visitors are allowed to climb the tower's eighty-five steps to the lantern room, where the station's three-and-a-half-order lens sits ready to beam its warning out across the lake. The classic prismatic lens focuses light into a brilliant beacon visible from a distance of more than a dozen miles. Lenses of this type were invented during the 1820s by a French scientist named Fresnel. The Sturgeon Point Fresnel lens is of an unusual size and shape designed especially for use on the Great Lakes.

TO SEE THE LIGHT: To reach the lighthouse, take US 23 north from Harrisville, then follow Lakeshore Drive and Point Road to Sturgeon Point. The parking lot is less than a mile down the road. The museum is open daily from Memorial Day to Labor Day and Friday through Sunday through the end of October. For information visit http://theenchantedforest.com/Alcona HistoricalSociety.

Location: Alcona

Established: 1870

Tower height: 68 feet

Elevation of the focal plane: 69 feet

Optic: Fresnel (third-order)

Status: Active

Characteristic: Flashes every 6 seconds

Range: 14 miles

Position: 44° 42' 42
83° 16' 18

Note: Marks a killer reef

ALPENA LIGHT

Across the Thunder Bay River from the old Lake Huron port city of Alpena, a spindly-legged, red metal tower marks the end of the harbor breakwater. Since the middle of the twentieth century, when Russian space capsules first circled the planet, the little skeleton tower has been known affectionately as "Sputnik." Although unlikely to blast off into the void, the tower is able to dazzle mariners with its flashing red light, just as it has since 1914.

TO SEE THE LIGHT: Although closed to the public, this little lighthouse can be seen from several points along the Alpena waterfront. Alpena is the site of the annual Great Lakes Lighthouse Festival held each October. Attended by authors, historians, experts, and vendors from across America, this is probably the finest and most popular lighthouse event in the United States. For festival information contact (989) 595–3632 or www.lighthousefestival.org.

Location: Alpena

Established: 1914

Tower height: 44 feet

Elevation of the focal plane: 44 feet

Optic: Modern

Status: Active

Characteristic: Flashes red every 5 seconds

Range: 14 miles

Position: 45° 03' 36 83° 25' 24

Note: Known affectionately as "Sputnik"

Established in 1905, the Middle Island Light was automated and abandoned by the Coast Guard years ago. However, thanks to a hardworking group of lighthouse preservationists, this handsome 71-foot island tower north of Alpena is being restored to tip-top condition. Known as the Middle Island Light Keepers Association, the group hopes to open the station to guests as a bed-and-breakfast inn.

TO SEE THE LIGHT: The lighthouse is accessible by boat. Contact the Middle Island Light Keepers Association, 5671 Rockport Road, Alpena, MI 49707; (989) 595–3600 May through October; the rest of the year (989) 595–3632. This group helps sponsor and organize the Great Lakes Lighthouse Festival held each October in Alpena.

Location: Near Alpena

Established: 1905

Tower height: 71 feet

Elevation of the focal plane: 78 feet

Optic: Modern

Status: Active

Characteristic: Flashes every 10 seconds

Range: 17 miles

Position: 45° 11' 36
83° 19' 18

Note: Handsome station restored by local preservationists

Bob and Sandra Shanklin,
The Lighthouse People

PRESQUE ISLE LIGHT (OLD AND NEW)

A treasure trove of lighthouses awaits visitors at Presque Isle, home to no fewer than four light towers. The oldest, a 30-foot stone-and-brick structure now known as Old Presque Isle Lighthouse, served the peninsula from 1840 to 1871. During the Civil War a pair of range lights marked the channel for vessels bound in and out of the harbor. In addition, President Abraham Lincoln authorized construction of a new, higher light tower at the main light station. The New Presque Isle Lighthouse took several years to complete and finally went into service in 1871. The 113-foot tower, one of the highest on the Great Lakes, still holds its original third-order Fresnel lens. Its beacon is visible from up to 20 miles away.

Location: Presque Isle

Established: 1871

Tower height: 113 feet

Elevation of the focal plane: 123 feet

Optic: Fresnel (third-order)

Status: Active

Characteristic: Flashes every 10 seconds

Range: 20 miles

Position: 45° 21' 24 83° 29' 30

Note: Replaced an earlier structure built in 1840

The lantern room atop the tall (new) Presque Isle tower contains a classic third-order Fresnel lens, which has focused the station's bright beacon since 1871.

Although taken out of service when its much taller neighbor was completed in 1871, the original (Old) Presque Isle Lighthouse still stands. It is said that the spirit of a former keeper still climbs the old tower's stone stairs.

The Old and New Presque Isle Light towers and the two peninsula range lights now stand in neighborly proximity. The New Presque Isle Light sits amid a scenic one-hundred-acre park maintained by the Presque Isle Township. All four lighthouses are easily accessible and together give visitors an unusually complete look at the history of a light station.

TO SEE THE LIGHT: From Presque Isle, follow Grand Lake Road past the intersection of Highway 638, or from US 23, take Highway 638 to Grand Lake Road and turn left. The Old Presque Isle Lighthouse and Museum is just over a half mile to the north. The range light towers stand nearby. From the museum, continue north for about a mile on Grand Lake Road to New Presque Isle Lighthouse, where you'll find a second museum and gift shop; call (989) 595–9917. For the Old Presque Isle Lighthouse Museum, call (989) 595–6979.

FORTY MILE POINT LIGHT

One of the last dark stretches facing ships navigating the Great Lakes was finally lit when the Forty Mile Point Light beacon began to flash in 1897. Shining from a square brick tower equipped with a fourth-order Fresnel lens, the light guides vessels passing between Cheboygan and Presque Isle.

The architecturally interesting dwelling features two gables, one on either side of the light tower. A brick oil house and fog-signal building complete the station. Although well maintained, the tower, dwelling, and other structures are not open to the public at this time.

Nonetheless, the site is well worth a visit. The grounds and buildings are lovely, and the beach below the lighthouse features the hulk of a wooden ship that wrecked here long ago. Visitors often walk the beach looking for pudding stones, the remnants of a volcanic eruption many millions of years ago.

TO SEE THE LIGHT: Drive about 6 miles north of Rogers City on US 23. Look for a sign pointing the way to Presque Isle County Lighthouse Park. Turn right onto an otherwise unmarked road and follow it to the lighthouse (do not take Forty Mile Point Road).

Location: Rogers City

Established: 1897

Tower height: 53 feet

Elevation of the focal plane: 66 feet

Optic: Fresnel (fourth-order)

Status: Active

Characteristic: Flashes every 6 seconds

Range: 16 miles

Position: 45° 29' 12
83° 54' 48

Note: Stands approximately 40 nautical miles from the Straits of Mackinac

MICHIGAN REEF LIGHTS

During the late nineteenth century, the growth of shipping on the Great Lakes focused attention on the Straits of Mackinac, the link connecting Lake Huron to Lake Michigan. Here Huron narrows to a mere few miles in width, forcing ships to run a gauntlet of treacherous shallows and killer reefs. Some thought—and many still believe—this to be the most treacherous stretch of water of the Great Lakes. To make navigation safer, the government marked threatening obstacles with lighthouses, some of them built in open water directly over the shoals. These became vital in the nearly thousand-mile-long chain of navigational markers that now guide freighters from the Atlantic deep into the heart of the North American continent.

After the submerged claws of Spectacle Reef hooked a pair of large schooners in 1867, Congress approved funds to mark the shoal with a lighthouse. The job took $406,000 and two hundred men working nearly four years, but by 1874 the Spectacle Reef Lighthouse was at last complete. Its beacon, now solar-powered, still warns ships. The Poe Reef Lighthouse (1929) remains in operation, as does the Detour Reef Lighthouse (1931), now undergoing extensive restoration. All are now automated. These reef lighthouses are not open to the public, and most are difficult to view from land.

Location: Lake Huron

Established: 1874

Tower height: 93 feet

Elevation of the focal plane: 86 feet

Optic: Modern (solar-powered)

Status: Active

Characteristic: Flashes red every 5 seconds

Range: 11 miles

Position: 45° 46' 24 84° 08' 12

Note: Open-water station took nearly 4 years to complete

Bob and Sandra Shanklin, The Lighthouse People

Spectacle Reef Light

TO SEE THE LIGHTS: Although they can be seen at a distance from land or enjoyed up close from the water, Michigan's reef lighthouses are off-limits to the public.

Bob and Sandra Shanklin, The Lighthouse People

Poe Reef Light

Location: Lake Huron

Established: 1929

Tower height: 60 feet

Elevation of the focal plane: 71 feet

Optic: Modern

Status: Active

Characteristic: Flashes white every 2 seconds

Range: 9 miles

Position: 45° 41' 42
84° 21' 42

Note: Square tower built atop a concrete caisson

Bob and Sandra Shanklin, The Lighthouse People

Detour Reef Light

Location: Near DeTour Village

Established: 1931

Tower height: 63 feet

Elevation of the focal plane: 74 feet

Optic: Modern

Status: Active

Characteristic: Flashes every 10 seconds

Range: 18 miles

Position: 45° 56' 54
83° 54' 12

Note: Declared obsolete by Coast Guard but saved by lighthouse preservationists

ROUND ISLAND LIGHT

Built in 1895, the brick Round Island Light was all but abandoned by the Coast Guard decades ago. Located on an exposed spit, the structure rapidly deteriorated, and at one point storm-driven waves were washing directly into the structure. Undercut by erosion, the old lighthouse seemed certain to collapse. Then the lighthouse was featured in the hit movie *Somewhere in Time*, a melo-drama starring the late Christopher Reeve. The attention attracted by the movie won new friends for the lighthouse, and preservationists started looking for ways to save it. Tourists visiting the nearby Mackinac Island resort community were asked to contribute, and in time the erosion was stopped and the historic lighthouse restored.

TO SEE THE LIGHT: The Round Island Lighthouse is not open to the public, but an excellent view can be had from the decks of ferries approaching or leaving Mackinac Island. It is worth making the trip just to see the lighthouse. However, Mackinac Island has countless charms of its own. Among them are the magnificent Grand Hotel and the fact that no auto-mobiles are allowed on the island. Passengers and freight are transported in carts pulled by draft horses. For ferry information call the Arnold Line at (906) 643–8275, the Star Line at (800) 638–9892, or Shepler's Mackinac Island Ferry at (800) 828–6157.

Location: Near Mackinac Island

Established: 1895

Tower height: 53 feet

Elevation of the focal plane: 53 feet

Optic: Modern (solar-powered)

Status: Private aid to navigation

Characteristic: Flashes red every 5 seconds

Range: 14 miles

Position: 45° 50' 36
84° 36' 54

Note: Saved after it appeared in a hit movie

CHEBOYGAN CRIB LIGHT

Location: Cheboygan

Established: 1910

Tower height: 25 feet

Elevation of the focal plane: Not known

Optic: Fresnel (removed)

Status: Deactivated 1988

Note: Now part of a Cheboygan city park

Barely two stories tall, the octagonal Cheboygan Crib Light tower looks a little like a chessboard rook. It once stood on an offshore crib, hence the name. A crib is an open water foundation constructed by filling an enormous wooden box with stone or concrete. But the light was moved ashore after it was deactivated in 1988. It is now the primary attraction of a small lakefront city park in Cheboygan.

TO SEE THE LIGHT: The lighthouse stands on the landward end of a pier extending into Lake Huron from Cheboygan's Gordon Turner Park, just off Huron Street. The tower is not open to the public, but visitors are welcome to walk the grounds. The Cheboygan Range Light is located a short distance away.

Location: Cheboygan

Established: 1880

Tower height: 45 feet

Elevation of the focal plane: 45 feet

Optic: Locomotive lantern

Status: Active

Characteristic: Fixed red

Range: Not known

Position: 45° 38' 51
84° 28' 22

Note: Distinguished by two enormous vertical red stripes

Like most other range lights, this one was designed to guide vessels into a narrow harbor approach channel. However, the front-range light was discontinued many years ago, and the existing structure now serves alone, primarily as a daymark. A pair of vertical red stripes on the front of the wooden tower help approaching navigators keep their bearings.

TO SEE THE LIGHT: The lighthouse is located near Cheboygan's Gordon Turner Park, just off Huron Street. The station is not open to the public.

MACKINAC POINT LIGHT

The original Mackinaw City station opened in 1890 as a fog-signal station. It was, obviously, much needed. During one amazingly foggy two-week stretch, hardworking stokers burned fifty-two cords of wood to keep its boilers filled with steam.

By late 1892 a lighthouse was ready to supplement the fog signal, and the 40-foot tower, equipped with a fourth-order lens, began a stint of service that ended only after the 1957 bridge opened up. Today the buff-colored station, with its bright red roof, is part of a historical park run by the Mackinac Island State Park Commission.

In 1957 a bridge over Mackinac Straits opened, making the Old Mackinac Point Light obsolete. Vessels began taking bearings

from the long string of bridge lights, and the beacon at the top of the turn-of-the-century station was soon turned off. Within three years the building had been converted into a maritime museum.

TO SEE THE LIGHT: Take Interstate 75 to exit 336. Follow Nicolet Avenue through Mackinaw City and turn right onto Huron Avenue. The Old Mackinac Point Light parking area is about 2 blocks down Huron Avenue. The lighthouse sits in a park that overlooks the Mackinac Bridge. Picnic tables and lovely surroundings will tempt you to make this a leisurely stop. The lighthouse is open to the public from mid-May to early October as a restoration-in-progress. For information call (231) 436–4100.

Location: Mackinaw City

Established: 1892

Tower height: 40 feet

Elevation of the focal plane: Not known

Optic: Fresnel (fourth-order)

Status: Deactivated 1957

Note: Marked the narrowest point of the Mackinac Straits

CHAPTER TWO:
LIGHTS ALONG LAKE MICHIGAN

Among the thousands of vessels lost in the Great Lakes was the very first European-style trading ship to sail these waters. In 1679 the French explorer Sieur de La Salle and a party of fur traders built a 50-ton sailing ship, pushing her off into Lake Erie from a rough-hewn shipyard where the city of Buffalo now stands. This was no crude, overbuilt canoe. Christened the *Griffon*, she was more than 60 feet long and had five cannons arrayed below the deck. The *Griffon* was intended to make La Salle and his fellow adventurers rich when they filled her holds with muskrat and beaver pelts gathered by French and Native American trappers.

The *Griffon* proved a worthy ship, weathering more than one fierce storm on the outbound leg of her maiden voyage to the far reaches of the Great Lakes. Still in 1679, La Salle disembarked to continue his explorations (while doing so, he discovered the upper Mississippi River). As he watched the *Griffon* sail away eastward, he was confident that the ship and her treasured cargo of furs would safely reach their destination. But neither the *Griffon* nor her crew was ever heard from again. Probably, like the *Fitzgerald* and so many other unlucky ships, she was smashed by a sudden, sharp autumn gale. It was an unfortunate, and ominous, beginning for commercial shipping on the Great Lakes.

Nearly 300 years later, in November 1958, the 640-foot *Carl D. Bradley* was heading home empty, making her last run of the fall shipping season. She had left behind in Buffington, Indiana, her cargo of some 18,000 tons of limestone, enough rock to fill 300 railroad cars. As the *Bradley* approached the top of Lake Michigan, less than a day's sail from her home port of Rogers City, Michigan, she ran straight into one of the lake's proverbial November storms.

Wind whipped across the deck at upward of 70 miles per hour, and 30-foot waves slammed into the bow. But for the *Bradley*'s thirty-five officers and crew, all hardened veterans of furious lake tempests, confronting such ugly weather was simply part of a day's work. Despite the pitching and rolling, no one got seasick, as the men wolfed down their dinner of hamburgers, french fries, and sponge cake.

Groaning under the strain placed on them by the huge waves, some of the hull plates began to shear off rivets and shoot them like bullets across the empty hold. Except for anyone unlucky enough to be caught in the line of fire, this was no particular cause for alarm. It was, in fact, a common experience in a storm.

But a loud booming sound caught the attention of the entire crew just after 5:30 P.M. It was not something any of them had heard before. The boom was followed moments later by another, then another. Captain Roland Bryan and First Mate Elmer Fleming looked back from the pilothouse and, to their horror, saw the aft section of the *Bradley* begin to sag. The ship was breaking in half!

Immediately, Captain Bryan sounded a general alarm, and Fleming put out a call over the ship's radiophone to all within hearing: "Mayday! Mayday!" For the *Carl D. Bradley* and nearly all of her crew, however, it was already too late.

Less than a quarter of an hour after the first sign of trouble, the *Bradley's* bow and stern sections parted and, within minutes, went their separate ways to the bottom. Those crewmen not carried down with the ship were left to fight for their lives on the wildly tossing surface. In those brutal, 36° waters, it was a struggle they could not hope to win. If they could see through the storm the lighthouse beacons from nearby Beaver Island, Cat Head, or elsewhere along the Michigan coast, it must have been a bitter reminder that safe ground was so near and yet so far away. One after another of the *Bradley's* crew froze to death or gave up and disappeared into the dark water.

The first would-be rescue ship to arrive over the *Bradley's* watery grave was a small German freighter, the *Christian Sartori*. No survivors could be located. The *Sartori* found only an eerie scattering of wave-tossed debris. The *Sartori's* captain and crew searched diligently, soon concluding that all hands had been lost; but as it turned out, they were wrong. Incredibly, some fourteen hours after the big stone carrier broke apart, a U.S. Coast Guard helicopter searching the open waters of Lake Michigan spotted an orange raft. Not long afterward the crew of the cutter *Sundew* pulled aboard First Mate Fleming and Frank Mays, a young deck watchman. These two alone remained alive to tell the story of the *Carl D. Bradley's* last day on the lake.

SOUTH MANITOU ISLAND LIGHT

Location: South Manitou Island (Lake Michigan)

Established: 1839

Tower height: 104 feet

Elevation of the focal plane: 100 feet

Optic: Fresnel (removed)

Status: Decommissioned in 1958

Note: Now an attraction of Sleeping Bear Dunes National Lakeshore

Among the most impressive structures on the Great Lakes is the conical tower of South Manitou Island Light. Soaring 104 feet into the skies over Lake Michigan, its stark white walls now seem a natural part of the pristine island that surrounds them. The tower and keeper's dwelling have been empty since 1958, when the Coast Guard decommissioned the station. Handsomely restored by the U.S. Park Service, they are now part of the Sleeping Bear Dunes National Lakeshore.

Built in 1872 to replace an early structure (possibly from 1839), this grand lighthouse once marked the Manitou Passage for ships navigating the tricky Mackinac Straits. Its powerful light, seen from a distance of 18 miles, was produced by a third-order Fresnel lens.

Incidentally, the islands are still marked by an active navigational light. Known as the North Manitou Island Shoal Light, this open-water station is far less attractive and historically significant than its neighbor on South Manitou Island.

TO SEE THE LIGHT: To reach the South Manitou Island Light, take the ferry from Leland, on the mainland. For schedules and prices, call (231) 256–9061. Passengers get a good view of the North Manitou Island Shoal Light (1935) during the passage. The South Manitou Island Light is a short hike from the ferry slip. The Sleeping Bear Dunes National Lakeshore offices can be reached at (231) 326–5134.

Well north of the Manitou Islands is historic Beaver Island, where radical Mormon James Jesse Strang at one time reigned as a self-styled king. He had already been deposed by 1858, when the original light was replaced by the 46-foot-high, yellow-brick Beaver Island Light and its attached two-story keeper's dwelling.

The Beaver Island station was once a popular destination for picnickers, who rode sleighs over the winter ice from Charlevoix, on the mainland. Occasionally, even cars made the trip. In 1929 three Model T Fords set out for the island, only to get lost in the fog. The resident keeper finally guided them to safety with the station's fog bell. The Coast Guard kept the light in operation until 1962. At present the building serves a different use: It is now an environmental education center for Charlevoix County public schools.

TO SEE THE LIGHT: A ferry from Charlevoix provides access to Beaver Island. The three-hour ride can be expensive. For schedules and prices, call (231) 547–2311.

Location: Beaver Island

Established: 1851

Tower height: 46 feet

Elevation of the focal plane: 103 feet

Optic: Fresnel (fourth-order, removed)

Status: Deactivated 1962

Note: Now operated as a special school for disadvantaged students

U.S. Coast Guard

ST. HELENA ISLAND LIGHT

Established in 1873, the St. Helena Island Light served ships passing through the Mackinac Straits. Automated in 1922, the 71-foot brick tower and attached dwelling suffered greatly from neglect and vandalism. It might have fallen into ruin, but believing it deserved a better fate, the Great Lakes Lighthouse Keepers Association has begun the formidable task of repairing and caring for the structure. Michigan Boy Scouts can earn Eagle Scout badges by helping with restoration work.

TO SEE THE LIGHT: St. Helena Island can be reached by boat from St. Ignace. For information on the lighthouse restoration project, write to Great Lakes Lighthouse Keepers Association, P.O. Box 580, Allen Park, MI 48101, or call (313) 662–1200.

Location: St. Helena Island near the Straits of Mackinac

Established: 1873

Tower height: 71 feet

Elevation of the focal plane: 71 feet

Optic: Modern (solar-powered)

Status: Active

Characteristic: Flashes every 6 seconds

Range: 6 miles

Position: 45° 51' 18 84° 51' 46

Note: Michigan Boy Scouts have helped restore the station

A narrow, mile-long channel links the pristine waters of Lake Charlevoix to Lake Michigan. Ferries, Coast Guard patrol boats, and other vessels are guided in and out of the channel by the red flash of the Charlevoix Lighthouse beacon. Established in 1885, the original wooden tower was replaced by the current metal structure in 1948.

TO SEE THE LIGHT: Charlevoix is located on U.S. Highway 31 about 50 miles north of Traverse City. A parking area off Grant Street provides a good view of the lighthouse.

Location: Charlevoix

Established: 1885

Tower height: 30 feet

Elevation of the focal plane: 41 feet

Optic: Modern (solar-powered)

Status: Active

Characteristic: Flashes red every 4 seconds

Range: 10 miles

Position: 45° 19' 13
85° 15' 53

Note: Marks the entrance to scenic Lake Charlevoix

Location: Near Traverse City

Established: 1870

Tower height: 40 feet

Status: Deactivated 1933

Note: Serves as the primary attraction of a local historical park

Interestingly, this light station is located on the forty-fifth parallel, exactly halfway between the North Pole and the equator. Most of the mariners who depended on this light, however, were more keenly interested in the fact that the Mission Point beacon marked the far end of the slender—and sometimes dangerous—peninsula that divides Traverse Bay. Established in 1870, the station was deactivated in 1933. Nowadays, the combination wooden tower and dwelling serve as the central attraction of a local park.

TO SEE THE LIGHT: From Traverse City, follow Highway 37 north to its end, where a small historical park surrounds the lighthouse. The building is closed to the public, but visitors may walk the grounds at their leisure.

Built in 1852 on strategic Cat Head Point, this lighthouse commanded the entrance to Grand Traverse Bay, guiding ships with a beacon produced by a relatively small fourth-order Fresnel lens. The light beamed out into the lake from atop a square tower that rose just above the roofline of a large, two-story brick dwelling. After serving mariners for more than a century, the old lighthouse was retired in 1972, its duties taken over by a nearby skeleton tower. The structure currently houses an excellent lighthouse museum. Among its exhibits is a fourth-order Fresnel lens.

TO SEE THE LIGHT: The lighthouse is located in Leelanau State Park, at the end of a long peninsula pointing northward into Lake Michigan. From Traverse City, follow Highway 22 to Northport and then County Road 201 to the park. Contact the Grand Traverse Lighthouse Museum at (231) 386–7195.

Location: Northport

Established: 1852

Tower height: 47 feet

Elevation of the focal plane: 50 feet

Status: Deactivated 1972

Note: Now houses a fine lighthouse museum

POINT BETSIE LIGHT

Built in 1858 to mark a key turning place for ships moving in or out of the strategic Manitou Passage, the Point Betsie Light has long been considered among the most important navigational aids on the Great Lakes. The original 37-foot tower and attached two-story dwelling still stand, and the light still shines each night. The Point Betsie Light was among the last light stations on the Great Lakes to be automated. Resident keepers operated the light until 1983, when electronic machinery took over the job.

For more than a century, Lake Michigan's often angry waters have chopped away at Point Betsie, eroding the beach as if determined to reclaim the land from the keepers and Coast Guard personnel. To slow the steadily advancing lake waters and save the structure, the government has erected steel breakwaters and concrete abutments. A broad concrete apron pushes out from the base of the tower to the edge of the lake. The lighthouse now seems stable enough, but in a storm the walls shudder when the waves crash onto the apron.

TO SEE THE LIGHT: Used as a private residence, the lighthouse is not open to the public but can be viewed from Point Betsie Road, off Highway 22 about 5 miles north of Frankfort.

Location: Frankfort

Established: 1858

Tower height: 37 feet

Elevation of the focal plane: 52 feet

Optic: Modern

Status: Active

Characteristic: Flashes every 10 seconds

Range: 19 miles

Position: 44° 21' 29
86° 15' 19

Note: The last Lake Michigan light to be automated (1983)

Rick Polad

FRANKFORT NORTH BREAKWATER LIGHT

rankfort and its lighthouse are located a few miles south of Point Betsie where the southwest-trending Michigan shoreline bends due south. One of many pier or breakwater lights dotting the eastern shore of Lake Michigan, the Frankfort North Breakwater Light has guided vessels in and out of the harbor since 1873. A white, pyramidal steel tower, it stands out near the end of the breakwater where it can be seen for miles by vessels moving up or down

Location: Frankfort

Established: 1873

Tower height: 72 feet

Elevation of the focal plane: 67 feet

Optic: Modern

Status: Active

Characteristic: Fixed

Range: 16 miles

Position: 44° 37' 54 86° 15' 06

Note: This tall, steel tower has stood up to countless storms

the Michigan coast. In this exposed position, it is frequently pounded by storm-driven waves, but it has successfully resisted them for more than a century.

TO SEE THE LIGHT: The lighthouse is closed to the public, but it can be seen from the western end of Main Street in Frankfort, which is located about 20 miles north of Manistee on Highway 22.

BIG SABLE POINT LIGHT

The construction of the 112-foot Big Sable Point Light in 1867 helped fill one of the last dark stretches along the western Michigan shore. The light, originally produced by a third-order Fresnel lens, helped coast-hugging vessels avoid the point and reach Ludington safely. So did the station's powerful foghorn, which proved quite a bit more efficient than its predecessor.

During its early days Ludington's unusual fog signal consisted of a metal horn made in the shape of a long bugle, which stood beside a train track. Whenever a blanket of fog rolled in from the lake, citizens brought a steam locomotive right up to the tongue of the horn and periodically gave a blast on its whistle. Magnified by the horn, the train whistle could be heard for many miles out on the lake.

Wind and weather hammered away at the tower's brick walls, and by the 1920s the lighthouse was in danger of collapse. To protect it, officials had the tower encased in a shell of riveted iron plates. Painted in broad white and black bands, the Big Sable Point tower is one of the most distinctive structures on the Great Lakes. Now part of Ludington State Park, the station remains in operation.

TO SEE THE LIGHT: From U.S. Highway 10 in Ludington, turn right onto Lakeshore Drive and follow it for approximately 6 miles to Ludington State Park. The lighthouse can be reached via a ½-mile walk up the beach from the parking lot. Also in the area is the Ludington Pierhead Light, which can be reached by following Ludington Avenue to Stearns Park. Built in the early twentieth century, it stands on a concrete base that looks something like the bow of a ship. For information call (231) 845–7343.

Location: Ludington

Established: 1867

Tower height: 112 feet

Elevation of the focal plane: 106 feet

Optic: Modern

Status: Active

Characteristic: Fixed white

Range: 15 miles

Position: 44° 03' 30
86° 30' 54

Note: Brick tower is protected from the weather by a shell of iron plates

LUDINGTON NORTH BREAKWATER LIGHT

Location: Ludington

Established: 1871

Tower height: 57 feet

Elevation of the focal plane: 55 feet

Optic: Modern

Status: Active

Characteristic: Flashes every 6 seconds

Range: 9 miles

Position: 43° 57' 12
88° 28' 12

Note: A familiar sight to cross-lake ferry passengers

This white, steel pyramidal tower marks the end of the breakwater protecting Pere Marquette Harbor near Ludington. The harbor and its lighthouse are located about halfway between the famous light stations at Big Sable Point to the north and Little Sable Point to the south. Each evening during warm weather months, the Ludington North Breakwater Light guides into harbor the Lake Michigan Carferry operating between Ludington and Manitowoc, Wisconsin, on the far side of the lake.

TO SEE THE LIGHT: The lighthouse is not open to the public but can be seen from Stearns Park at the western end of Ludington Avenue (US 10) in Ludington. Passengers on the Lake Michigan Carferry get an excellent view of the tower. For more information on the ferry or to make reservations, call (800) 841–4243.

LITTLE SABLE POINT LIGHT

When completed in 1874, the tower at Little Sable Point was nearly a twin of its sister lighthouse at Big Sable Point. Both towers stood 107 feet tall, both were constructed of brick, and both were fitted with third-order Fresnel lenses. But unlike its neighbor, which was eventually covered in steel plates, the Little Sable tower still looks much the way it did more than 130 years ago.

The keeper's dwelling was demolished when the station was automated in the 1950s, leaving the tower to stand a solitary vigil. One of the loveliest lighthouses on Lake Michigan, its redbrick walls offer a handsome contrast to the white dunes of Silver Lake State Park. The station's original Fresnel lens remains in use.

TO SEE THE LIGHT: From US 31 near Mears, turn west on Shelby Road and follow the signs to Silver Lake State Park. For the nearby White River Lighthouse (1875), turn west off US 31 on White Lake Road, then follow South Shore Road and Murray Road.

Location: Near Mears

Established: 1874

Tower height: 107 feet

Elevation of the focal plane: 108 feet

Optic: Fresnel (third-order)

Status: Active

Characteristic: Flashes every 6 seconds

Range: 17 miles

Position: 43° 39' 09
86° 32' 24

Note: Oldest brick lighthouse on the Great Lakes

WHITE RIVER LIGHTHOUSE

During the years after the Civil War, Michigan's forest industries burgeoned and the area around Muskegon became known as the Lumber Queen of the World. Most of the lumber produced in this part of the state was floated down rivers to small ports such as Whitehall, where it was loaded onto freighters and shipped to markets in the east. In 1875 a light station was built at Whitehall to guide the lumber freighters in and out of harbor. Known as the White River Lighthouse, it consisted of a 40-foot octagonal tower and attached keeper's dwelling, both built of Michigan limestone. Captain William Robinson, the station's first keeper, served here for almost half a century. The U.S. Coast Guard deactivated the beacon in 1960, and the lighthouse eventually became an engaging maritime museum. Known today as the White River Lighthouse Museum, it sheds light on Michigan's rich nautical tradition.

TO SEE THE LIGHT: Driving along US 31 north of Muskegon, take the White River Drive exit and proceed west to South Shore Drive. Turn left and follow signs to the lighthouse and museum. For hours and other information, call (231) 894–8265.

Location: Whitehall

Established: 1875

Tower height: 38 feet

Elevation of the focal plane: 42 feet

Status: Decommissioned 1960

Note: The station's first keeper served for 47 years

MUSKEGON SOUTH PIERHEAD LIGHT

The eastern shores of Lake Michigan are marked by several of the most beautiful and distinctive pier lighthouses in America. Located on often lengthy stone or concrete piers that place them well out in the lake, these towers guide vessels in and out of harbors and warn them away from the piers and other dangerous obstacles. Many of the Michigan pier lighthouses were built during a flurry of construction in the early 1900s.

As is the case with several of these offshore towers, the Muskegon South Pierhead Light is painted bright red for better daytime visibility. And it's covered in iron to stand up to the lake's pounding waves. Built in 1903, the tower is 53 feet high, and its lantern holds a modern optic lens. The tower and its light guide vessels through the passage that links Muskegon Lake with the open waters of Lake Michigan.

TO SEE THE LIGHT: In Muskegon take Sherman Boulevard to Beach Street and follow it to Pere Marquette Park. The pier and light are located just north of the park, which offers excellent swimming and picnicking.

Location: Muskegon

Established: 1903

Tower height: 53 feet

Elevation of the focal plane: 70 feet

Optic: Modern

Status: Active

Characteristic: Flashes red every 4 seconds

Range: 10 miles

Position: 43° 13' 36
86° 20' 29

Note: A bright red cast-iron cylinder

GRAND HAVEN PIER LIGHTS

Among the most striking of Michigan's pier lighthouses are those that mark the entrance to Grand Haven River, which offers one of the state's best deepwater harbors. Known as the Grand Haven South Pierhead Inner Light and Pier Light, they stand several hundred feet apart on a long stone pier. The inner tower, which was built in 1895, consists of a 51-foot steel cylinder topped by a small lantern. The squat pierhead tower was originally the station's fog-signal building and was moved to its present location when the pier was extended in 1905. A tiny lantern nestles on the roof. The towers have been sheathed in iron to protect them from the lake's destructive, storm-driven waves.

TO SEE THE LIGHTS: From US 31 in Grand Haven, follow
Franklin Avenue and South Harbor Drive to Grand Haven State Park.
The pier is open to the public and attracts droves of fishermen. The
park also offers picnicking and swimming.

When you're in the area, plan also to visit the Holland Harbor
(Black Lake) Light (1936) and South Haven Light (1903).

Location: Grand Haven

Established: 1905

Tower height: (Inner) 51
feet, (outer) 36 feet

Elevation of the focal
plane: (Inner) 52 feet,
(outer) 42 feet

Optic: Modern

Status: Active

Characteristics: (Inner)
red, occulting every
4 seconds; (outer)
flashes red every 10
seconds

Range: (Inner) 4 miles;
(outer) 15 miles

Position: 43° 03' 25
86° 15' 22

Note: The lakeside face
of the outer tower is
shaped like the bow of a
ship

HOLLAND HARBOR (BLACK LAKE) LIGHT

When it was completed in 1936 (an earlier light tower stood here as early as 1872), the existing Holland Harbor Light was sheathed in steel, and no wonder. Located at the end of a long pier, the little 32-foot structure takes a tremendous pounding during heavy weather. The tower rises through the slate roof of the main station building.

TO SEE THE LIGHT: In Holland turn west onto Douglas Avenue/Ottawa Beach Road and drive approximately 6 miles to Holland State Park. For information contact the West Michigan Tourist Association at (800) 442–2084.

Location: Holland

Established: 1872

Tower height: 32 feet

Elevation of the focal plane: 52 feet

Optic: Fresnel (sixth-order)

Status: Active

Characteristic: Alternates white and red at 10-second intervals

Range: 19 miles

Position: 42° 46' 22 86° 12' 45

Note: Impressive red tower, known as "Big Red," near the end of a pier

Bob and Sandra Shanklin, The Lighthouse People

South Haven seems just the sort of place to shop for antiques, and not surprisingly, this quaint lakeside community can boast its own antique lighthouse. Located at the far end of the harbor pier, the red cast-iron tower is still an active aid to navigation. Its original fifth-order Fresnel lens remains in place, warning mariners with a fixed red light.

TO SEE THE LIGHT: From US 31, follow Route 196 West, then Phoenix and Water Streets to South Haven's sandy beach. The lighthouse can be reached by walking a long concrete pier, but do not chance it in rough weather.

Location: South Haven

Established: 1872

Tower height: 35 feet

Elevation of the focal plane: 37 feet

Optic: Fresnel (fifth-order)

Status: Active

Characteristic: Fixed red

Range: 12 miles

Position: 42° 24' 06
86° 17' 18

Note: The station's former keeper's house is now owned by the city of South Haven

ST. JOSEPH NORTH PIER LIGHTS

Location: St. Joseph

Established: 1832

Tower height: (Inner) 53 feet; (outer) 30 feet

Elevation of the focal plane: (Inner) 53 feet; (outer) 31 feet

Optic: Fresnel (inner) fourth-order; (outer)fifth-order

Status: Active

Characteristic: (Inner) fixed; (outer) flashes every 6 seconds

Range: 15 miles

Position: 42° 07' 00 86° 29' 42

Note: This scenic station was featured on a postage stamp

Among the best known and loved of the Michigan pier lights are the St. Joseph Inner and Outer Pier Lighthouses, which function in tandem as range lights. As with all range lights, they are located some distance apart and are meant to be seen one atop the other. Mariners on the lake who see them in perpendicular alignment may rest assured that they are sailing in safe water.

A much earlier lighthouse, built on the mainland in 1832, served St. Joseph until it was discontinued during the 1920s; it was

eventually demolished. The St. Joseph North Pier Lights, established in 1907, still stand. The forward, or front-range, light is a cylindrical structure. The one closer to shore, or rear-range light, is octagonal. An elevated walkway links the two towers, each of which retains its original Fresnel lens.

TO SEE THE LIGHTS: From US 31 in St. Joseph, follow Marina Drive south to Tiscornia Park. The park offers an excellent view of both lights. Visitors who want a close look can walk out on the pier.

SAND POINT LIGHT

Vessels approaching Escanaba must take care to avoid Sand Point and a cluster of nearby shoals. To warn mariners away from these dangers, the government established a lighthouse on Sand Point in 1867. A fixed red light shone from the square brick tower, beaming toward the lake from just over 40 feet above the water.

The Coast Guard discontinued the light in 1939, after channel dredging rendered it obsolete. Coast Guard personnel used the building as a residence until 1985, when it was turned over to the Delta County Historical Society. Since then, the society has restored the Sand Point Light to its original appearance. The beacon, focused by a fourth-order Fresnel lens, is once again operational.

TO SEE THE LIGHT: Located in Ludington Park, just off U.S. Highways 2 and 41, the lighthouse (906–786–3763) is now a museum (906–786–3428).

Location: Escanaba

Established: 1867

Tower height: 41 feet

Elevation of the focal plane: 44 feet

Optic: Fresnel (fourth-order)

Status: Active

Characteristic: Flashes every 4 seconds

Range: 8 miles

Position: 46° 47' 06 88° 28' 00

Note: Reactivated in 1989 after 50 years of disuse

Rick Polad

Location: Manistique

Established: 1895

Tower height: 78 feet

Elevation of the focal plane: 80 feet

Optic: Aerobeacon

Status: Active

Characteristic: Flashes every 6 seconds

Range: 17 miles

Position: 45° 55' 18
85° 54' 42

Note: Marks one of the few good harbors on Lake Michigan's northwestern shore

One of only a few safe harbors on the north shore of Lake Michigan, Seul Choix was given its name, meaning "only choice," by early French explorers. Seul Choix Point Light stands guard over this inviting harbor. Even so, it did not receive a lighthouse until late in the nineteenth century. Congress finally appropriated money for the project in 1886, but partly because of its remote location, the lighthouse was not completed and operational until 1895.

The conical brick tower, 78 feet tall, was topped by a ten-sided, cast-iron lantern, giving its third-order Fresnel lens a focal plane just over 80 feet above the lake. When the Coast Guard automated the lighthouse, the Fresnel lens was removed and replaced by an airport-style beacon, visible from about 17 miles out in the lake.

The two-story brick keeper's dwelling still stands and is attached to the tower by an enclosed brick passageway. Although the structure and the grounds are now the property of the state of Michigan, this is still an operating light station.

TO SEE THE LIGHT: Turn off US 2 at Gulliver and follow Port Inland Road and then County Road 431 to the lighthouse. The tower and light are open daily from mid-May through mid-October. There is a small, but worthy, museum in the old fog-signal building. Contact the Gulliver Historical Society at R.R. 1, Box 79, Gulliver, MI 49840; (906) 283–3183.

CHAPTER THREE:
LIGHTS ALONG LAKE SUPERIOR

Sometimes lighthouses themselves were no less lonely, no less confining, no less at the mercy of the elements, than the ships they guided. The lighthouse keepers who once served at Lake Superior's remote outposts—places like Au Sable, Passage Island, and the Rock of Ages—were surely among the loneliest men and women in America, and the toughest.

Usually located at water's edge, lighthouses are exposed to the same heavy weather that tore at the ships on the lakes. But unlike ships, lighthouses cannot move, cannot be turned toward safe harbor, cannot remain tied up at the dock until the worst is over. In a storm they must stand their ground and take their beating, and during the days before lighthouse automation, their keepers had to do the same.

In the 1960s and 1970s, the Coast Guard automated the last manned lighthouses on the Great Lakes, including those on Superior. Afterward, their lamps and mechanisms operated by computers, photosensitive cells, and other "electronic keepers," the lake light-houses continued their vigil alone. In the past, however, their work had always required the help of human hands.

It is easy to imagine that lighthouse keepers were hermits, fugi-tives from noisy city streets and crowded factories who preferred a simpler, more peaceful life at water's edge. Generally speaking, however, that was not the case. Mostly they were ordinary Americans glad of the steady work and regular pay.

Keepers' salaries never amounted to much—often no more than $50 per month, and much less than that during the nineteenth century; but almost by definition, the job came with a house and an excellent view. Remote light stations were supplied with food, deliv-ered every few months by government lighthouse tenders, and usually there was a plot of ground where the keepers could grow vegetables and raise a few chickens. Many keepers lived with their families; some stations, though, such as the Rock of Ages Light, were much too isolated or too dangerous for family life.

Looking something like an enormous spark plug, the Rock of Ages Light rises from the open waters of Lake Superior about 5 miles off Isle Royale, itself one of the nation's most remote places. Nowadays, like all other Great Lakes lighthouses, the Rock of Ages Light is automated. But from 1908, the year it went into service, until the last resident crew left the station in 1977, the light was operated by a keeper and three assistants, who would remain on the Rock for up to eight months at a time. They arrived at the station in April and were taken ashore again in early December, when the thickening ice forced shipping off the lakes. The denizens of the Rock were allowed occasional shore leave on Isle Royale, but otherwise they lived at the station full time. In heavy weather no one could approach the station or leave it. If radio communication went down, the station crew could be cut off from all contact with the outside world.

Utterly barren, the Rock itself was only about 50 feet wide and supported not a single bush or blade of grass. Inside the 130-foot steel-plated tower, a spiral staircase offered access to a few small bunk rooms where the keepers slept; a galley and dining area where they ate; storage and equipment rooms where they worked; and, of course, the lantern room, with its huge second-order Fresnel lens. For the most part this was the keepers' whole world.

In 1931, in the midst of the Great Depression, a young Detroit reporter named Stella Champney sailed with the lighthouse tender *Marigold* as it made its semiannual visits to Lake Superior lighthouses. At the Rock of Ages Light, she interviewed first assistant keeper C. A. McKay.

McKay had had a terrifying experience only the year before. As a storm brewed out on the lake, his boss, keeper Emil Mueller, had fallen from the tower's spiral staircase and landed squarely on the bed where McKay was sleeping. McKay was uninjured, but Mueller lay dead of a heart attack.

McKay's explanation for the tragic incident was a simple one: "Too many steps. One room on top of another clear to the top. His heart gave out."

What was it like being out here in a storm? "You can't see anything but water," said McKay. "You can't hear anything but its roar. See that pier around the tower? It looks pretty high up and safe. Well, in a real storm, heavy, green water sweeps over it. You can't even see it sometimes. You can't get away from the water even at the top of the tower. Spray sweeps over the tower windows and, when it's very cold, freezes on the glass. You can't hear anything but the boom! boom! boom! of the seas as they sweep over the rocks, or the crack like gunfire as they hit the tower."

POINT IROQUOIS LIGHT

Point Iroquois gets its name from a massacre that took place here in 1662. A war party sent westward by the Iroquois Confederation was set upon and slaughtered on this point by an army of Ojibwas.

Ships passing by the point are also in danger of ambush. On their port side are the reefs near Gros Cap in Canada, while on their starboard side are the ship-killing rocks near Point Iroquois. The St. Marys River became a heavily trafficked thoroughfare after the Soo Locks connected Superior to the other lakes in 1855, and since that time many vessels have been lost while approaching the river. Often, an otherwise minor navigational error can be fatal here.

To help captains enter the river safely, a small lighthouse was built on Point Iroquois not long after the locks opened. Fitted with a sixth-order Fresnel lens, this modest wooden structure served until 1871, when it was replaced by an impressive 65-foot brick tower and dwelling that still stand today.

Its beacon discontinued in 1971, the lighthouse is now part of the Hiawatha National Forest. The handsome structures are maintained by the Bay Mills–Brimley Historical Research Society, which operates a museum and gift shop here.

TO SEE THE LIGHT: From Interstate 75, take Highway 28 for about 8 miles to the town of Brimley. Then follow Six Mile Road and Lakeshore Drive to the lighthouse. Original Lighthouse Service fixtures and nineteenth-century

Location: Near Sault Ste. Marie

Established: 1855

Tower height: 65 feet

Elevation of the focal plane: 68 feet

Optic: Fresnel (removed)

Status: Deactivated 1971

Note: Historic station has been handsomely restored

furnishings are on display. Contact the Point Iroquois Lighthouse and Maritime Museum, Sault Ste. Marie Ranger Office, 4000 I-75 Business Spur, Sault Ste. Marie, MI 49783; (906) 437-5272.

On the evening of November 10, 1975, the huge iron ore freighter *Edmund Fitzgerald* plowed through a powerful storm, heading for the relatively safe waters just beyond Whitefish Point. She never made it. The enormous ship, longer than two football fields, disappeared, along with twenty-nine crewmen, a few miles north of the point. The sinking of the *Edmund Fitzgerald* gave rise to a legend and a popular ballad by Gordon Lightfoot.

Ironically, on the night the *Big Fitz* met her end, the lighthouse on Whitefish Point was out of service. The storm had cut the power supply to the station. On thousands of other nights, however—almost continuously since 1849—mariners have been able to rely on the guidance of the station's beacon.

Recognizing the strategic nature of the point and its importance to shipping, the government established a light station here in 1849. Its masonry tower gave way to an iron-skeleton structure shortly before the Civil War. Braced by a network of iron supports, the tower's central steel cylinder is nearly 80 feet tall and topped by a metal lantern. The open design was intended to take stress off the building during high winds and storms like the one that sank the *Fitzgerald*. An interior spiral staircase provides access to the lantern room.

Automated in 1970, the station now serves as home to the Great Lakes Shipwreck Museum. Here imaginative visitors can relive the last moments of the *Fitzgerald* and many other ill-fated ships claimed forever by the lakes.

TO SEE THE LIGHT: The lighthouse and museum, housed in the former keeper's residence, can be reached from the Mackinac Bridge by taking I-75 north to Highway 123 and the town of Paradise. From Paradise, follow Whitefish Point Road to Whitefish Point. Call (888) 492-3747. The museum maintains an informative Web site: www.shipwreckmuseum.com.

Location: Paradise

Established: 1849

Tower height: 76 feet

Elevation of the focal plane: 80 feet

Optic: Aerobeacon

Status: Active

Characteristic: Flashes twice every 20 seconds

Range: 26 miles

Position: 46° 46' 18
84° 57' 24

Note: Oldest active lighthouse on the Great Lakes

CRISP POINT LIGHT

Veteran of nearly a century of service to mariners, the Crisp Point Light on Michigan's sparsely settled Upper Peninsula very nearly succumbed to the fate of far too many historic light towers. More or less abandoned by the government, it was all but

Location: West of Paradise

Established: 1904

Tower height: 58 feet

Elevation of the focal plane: 58 feet

Optic: Fresnel (removed)

Status: Deactivated 1993

Note: Recently saved from lakeshore erosion

destroyed by weather and erosion. Over the last decade, however, an idealistic couple, Don and Nellie Ross, has made saving the tower a personal crusade, and they have attained notable success. The advance of Lake Superior has been checked by a stone breakwater, and the lighthouse is slowly but surely being restored.

TO SEE THE LIGHT: Located 18 miles from the main road, a trip to Crisp Point is something of an adventure, but for those prepared to make the effort, it's a worthwhile one. Contact the Crisp Point Lighthouse Society, P.O. Box 229, Paradise, MI 49768; (906) 492–3206.

AU SABLE POINT LIGHT

For many years sailors dreaded the 80 miles of dark shoreline that stretched westward from Whitefish Point. Unmarked by any navigational light, these dangerous shores claimed dozens of ships. To fill the gap and save lives, a lighthouse was established on Au Sable Point in 1874.

The 86-foot brick tower was built on a rise, placing the beacon 107 feet above the surface of the lake. Its third-order Fresnel lens displayed a fixed white light. The attached, two-story dwelling was spacious, but the keepers who lived in it knew theirs was one of the most remote light stations in America. The nearest town, Grand Marais, lay more than 12 miles away, and there was no road. Keepers either hiked in or came by boat.

Perhaps because of its isolation, the Coast Guard automated the station in 1958, turning the property and buildings over to the National Park Service for inclusion in Pictured Rocks National Lakeshore.

TO SEE THE LIGHT: Just as keepers once did, visitors today must walk to this lighthouse, located in Pictured Rocks National Lakeshore on the Upper Peninsula. From Highway 28, take Highway 77 north for about 25 miles to Grand Marais. Then follow the gravel-surfaced Alger County Road H–58 for another 12 miles to the Hurricane Campground. There a trail provides access to the shore and the lighthouse. Write to Pictured Rocks National Lakeshore, P.O. Box 40, Munising, MI 49862, or call (906) 387–3700.

Location: Grand Marais

Established: 1874

Tower height: 86 feet

Elevation of the focal plane: 107 feet

Optic: Modern (solar-powered)

Status: Active

Characteristic: Flashes every 6 seconds

Range: 11 miles

Position: 46° 40' 18
86° 08' 24

Note: Located in Pictured Rocks National Lakeshore

MUNISING RANGE LIGHTS

Location: Munising

Established: 1908

Tower height: (front) 58
feet; (rear) 33 feet

Elevation of the focal
plane: (front) 79 feet;
(rear) 107 feet

Optic: Modern

Status: Active

Characteristic: Fixed
red (both)

Range: 10 miles
(approximate)

Position: 46° 24' 54
86° 39' 42

Note: Front tower is taller
than rear, a highly
unusual arrangement

For nearly a century the narrow, safe channel through Munising Bay has been marked by two extraordinary lighthouses. Unlike most range light structures, where the rear tower is taller, here the forward tower is by far the taller and more impressive of the two. The 58-foot steel front-range tower stands near the lakeshore, while the squat rear-range tower is located on a hillside some distance away. At night, both make their presence known with locomotive-style headlamps.

TO SEE THE LIGHTS: The Munising Front Range tower can be found just west of town off Route 28. The rear-range tower is a few blocks away at the end of Hemlock Street.

The shorter rear-range tower (above) sits on a hillside behind the taller front-range tower (right).

With the discovery of copper and iron in the mountains of the Upper Peninsula, Marquette became an important port. A lighthouse built here in 1853 guided ships into the city's harbor. Of poor construction quality, however, it lasted only a few years. The square masonry tower that replaced it in 1866 proved very much more durable and still serves to this day. A fourth-order classic lens at one time shone from atop the 40-foot tower, but an automated aeromarine beacon has taken its place.

TO SEE THE LIGHT: From U.S. Highway 41 in Marquette, follow Lake Street to the lighthouse. The tower is located on an active Coast Guard station. The nearby Marquette Maritime Museum offers occasional guided tours of the lighthouse; call (906) 226-2006.

Location: Marquette

Established: 1853

Tower height: 40 feet

Elevation of the focal plane: 77 feet

Optic: Aerobeacon

Status: Active

Characteristic: Flashes every 10 seconds

Range: 12 miles

Position: 46° 32' 48 87° 22' 36

Note: The bright red dwelling and tower visually dominate the harbor

BIG BAY LIGHT

Location: Big Bay

Established: 1896

Tower height: 65 feet

Elevation of the focal plane: 60 feet

Optic: Modern

Status: Active

Characteristic: Flashes every 6 seconds

Range: 11 miles

Position: 46° 50' 30 87° 40' 48

Note: Now doubles as a bed-and-breakfast inn

Many ships have foundered in the treacherous waters just to the north of the famed Huron Mountains. To help mariners find their way safely, the government established a major light at Big Bay in 1896. It shone from a square brick tower attached to a two-story dwelling. The light was automated shortly before World War II, and in 1961 it was moved to a nearby steel-skeleton tower. The old lighthouse was then converted for use as a private residence and later as a bed-and-breakfast inn.

TO SEE THE LIGHT: The inn is located on Lighthouse Road, about 3 miles north of Big Bay. Write to Big Bay Point Lighthouse, 3 Lighthouse Road, Big Bay, MI 49808, or call (906) 345–9957.

Winters on Michigan's Upper Peninsula are notoriously severe, but the weather did not deter the rapid development of mining when deposits of copper were found in the 1840s. The richest copper veins were located on the Keweenaw Peninsula, which thrusts to the northeast toward the center of Lake Superior. Ship traffic in and out of Copper Harbor expanded rapidly to carry the ore to markets in the east. Shippers and government officials soon saw the need for a lighthouse to guide the big freighters in and out of the harbor.

The stone tower with detached dwelling was located on a point near the harbor entrance. Upgraded and given a Fresnel lens in 1856, it was replaced with an entirely new structure shortly after the Civil War. A square stone tower with a small attached dwelling, this second Copper Harbor Light still stands, although its duties have been taken over by a beacon displayed from a nearby skeleton tower.

TO SEE THE LIGHT: The town of Copper Harbor is located at the far northern end of Route 26. The lighthouse is now part of Fort Wilkins State Park. It is best reached by water from Copper Harbor State Marina; call (906) 289–4966 Memorial Day through mid-October. Nearby is the wooden Copper Harbor Rear Range Lighthouse (1869). Far to the east of Copper Harbor, off the tip of the Keweenaw Peninsula, is the Manitou Island Lighthouse (1861). Its light, produced by a third-order Fresnel lens, remains active.

Location: Copper Harbor

Established: 1849

Tower height: 62 feet

Elevation of the focal plane: Not known

Optic: Fresnel (removed)

Status: Deactivated 1933

Note: Replaced by an automated light on a skeleton tower

EAGLE HARBOR LIGHT

Like Copper Harbor to the east, Eagle Harbor became a bustling ore-shipping point during the copper-and-iron boom years of the nineteenth and early twentieth centuries. From 1851 onward this important Keweenaw Peninsula port was marked by a key navigational light. During its first few years of service, the station was equipped with an outmoded lamp and reflector optic but received a Fresnel lens in 1857.

Lake Superior's notorious weather took a heavy toll on the lighthouse, and it lasted less than twenty years. The 44-foot octagonal tower and attached dwelling seen here today date from 1871. For many years the tower had a fourth-order Fresnel lens, but it was replaced by a modern aerobeacon in 1968, shortly before the station was automated.

TO SEE THE LIGHT: Follow Route 26 down the Keweenaw Peninsula and turn left toward the lake just before entering Eagle Harbor. The Keweenaw Historical Society, which has restored the station to its late-nineteenth-century appearance, maintains a nautical museum in one of the outer buildings. Call (906) 289–4990.

Location: Eagle Harbor

Established: 1851

Tower height: 44 feet

Elevation of the focal plane: 60 feet

Optic: Aerobeacon

Status: Active

Characteristic: Alternates red and white at 20-second intervals

Range: 28 miles

Position: 47° 27' 36 86° 09' 30

Note: The keeper's dwelling is said to be haunted

SAND HILLS LIGHT

Location: Near Eagle River

Established: 1919

Tower height: 91 feet

Elevation of the focal plane: More than 100 feet

Optic: Fresnel (removed)

Status: Deactivated 1954

Note: Now an elegant bed-and-breakfast

An imposing brick edifice with a square tower, the Sand Hills Lighthouse reflects the modernist style prevalent during the early twentieth century. The design is similar to that of Alaska's Scotch Cap Lighthouse, which was destroyed by a tsunami in the 1940s. Decommissioned by the Coast Guard in the 1950s, the building stood empty for decades, its interior all but gutted by time. Its walls remained solid, however, and a local lighthouse lover eventually bought the property. Handsomely restored, it is now an attractive lakeside inn.

TO SEE THE LIGHT: Located off Five Mile Point Road to the west of US 41, the Sand Hills Lighthouse Inn has eight delightful guest rooms. Reservations should be made far in advance; call (906) 337–1744.

Built in 1908 on an open-water caisson atop a notoriously dangerous shoal, the Rock of Ages Light was one of the most isolated manned light stations in America, if not the world. Keepers had to sail more than 50 miles across the often stormy waters of Lake Superior to spend a day in town, see a doctor, visit friends, or pick up food and supplies. For much of the year, the five-level, 130-foot-tall steel-plated light was their entire world.

In 1933 keepers had unexpected company when the freighter *George Cox* slammed into a nearby reef and sank. Rescued by the keeper and his assistant from the frigid waters of the lake, 125 survivors huddled in the lighthouse. They sat one atop the other on the tower's staircase until a ship arrived to take them to shore.

Anyone stranded on the rock nowadays would find nobody at home. The lighthouse has been automated since 1978, much to the relief, no doubt, of the lonely keepers. Following automation, the station lost its second-order classic lens, at one time the most powerful optic on the Great Lakes. A modern, 700,000-candlepower beacon shines here today.

TO SEE THE LIGHT: The Rock of Ages Light is closed to the public. It can sometimes be seen from the decks of ferries approaching Isle Royale.

Location: Near Isle Royale

Established: 1908

Tower height: 117 feet

Elevation of the focal plane: 130 feet

Optic: Modern

Status: Active

Characteristic: Flashes every 10 seconds

Range: 17 miles

Position: 47° 52' 01
89° 18' 49

Note: Construction of this lighthouse represented a major engineering feat

| # ROCK HARBOR LIGHT

Bob and Sandra Shanklin, The Lighthouse People

Location: Isle Royale

Established: 1855

Tower height: 50 feet

Elevation of the focal plane: 70 feet

Optic: Fresnel (removed)

Status: Deactivated 1879

Note: A key attraction of Isle Royale National Park

Now a pristine wilderness visited primarily by backpackers and outdoor enthusiasts, Isle Royale was, in the past, a thriving mining center. The discovery of copper here in the late 1840s led to construction of the Rock Harbor Light in 1855 to guide ore freighters to the island. The station consisted of a 50-foot brick tower with attached stone dwelling.

The Isle Royale copper veins played out within a few years, and by the late 1870s, mining ceased altogether. This made the Rock Harbor Light unnecessary, and it was closed permanently in 1879. The tower and dwelling still stand.

The work of guiding vessels and visitors to Isle Royale is handled nowadays by Isle Royale Lighthouse, located on a barren rock near the entrance to Siskit Bay. The stone tower, completed in 1875, still displays its white light, produced by a fourth-order Fresnel lens. Also still in operation is the Passage Island Lighthouse (1882), which marks the channel just off the northeastern tip of Isle Royale.

TO SEE THE LIGHT: For nature lovers—and lighthouse aficionados as well—a visit to Isle Royale National Park can be the experience of a lifetime. As many travelers can attest, however, reaching Isle Royale is no easy task. Usually, it requires a lengthy ferry ride from Copper Harbor or other departure points on the Upper Peninsula, and visitors must have prior reservations for camping or accommodations on the island. Contact Isle Royale National Park, 87 North Ripley Street, Houghton, MI 49931; (906) 482–0984.

PASSAGE ISLAND LIGHT

Now part of Isle Royale National Park, Passage Island Lighthouse is located on a remote island in Lake Superior. Since construction materials came at a premium to this faraway place, the laborers used stone gathered from the surface of the rocky island to build the octagonal tower and attached keeper's residence. Since commuting to the mainland was impossible, keepers lived here with their families much of the year then went ashore in winter when ice closed the lakes to navigation. The station was automated in 1978.

TO SEE THE LIGHT: Passage Island and its lighthouse are accessible only by boat. The best way to see and enjoy this historic station is through one of the tours offered during warm weather months by Isle Royale National Park; call (906) 482–0984.

Location: Passage Island (Lake Superior)

Established: 1882

Tower height: 44 feet

Elevation of the focal plane: 78 feet

Optic: Modern (solar-powered)

Status: Active

Characteristic: Flashes every 5 seconds

Range: 17 miles

Position: 48° 13' 24
88° 22' 00

Note: Michigan's oldest light station

GLOSSARY

Aids to Navigation Team

U.S. Coast Guard units assigned to operate and maintain light-houses, channel lights, buoys, and other maritime markers.

Automated light

A lighthouse with no keeper. Following World War II, remote control systems, light-activated switches, and fog-sensing devices made automation an increasingly cost-effective and attractive option, and the efficiency-minded U.S. Coast Guard automated one light station after another. By 1970, only about sixty U.S. lighthouses still had full-time keepers, and within two decades, all but one of those beacons had been automated. Appropriately enough, the historic Boston Harbor Lighthouse, automated in 1998, was the last to give up its keeper. All of Michigan's active lighthouses are now automated.

Beacon

A light or radio signal intended to guide mariners or aviators.

Breakwater or pier light

Often harbors are protected from high waves by a lengthy barrier of stone called a breakwater. Because they rise only a few feet above the surface, breakwaters are hard to see, especially at night, and may threaten vessels entering or exiting the harbor. Breakwater beacons are meant to make mariners aware of this hazard and safely navigate the harbor entrance. For obvious reasons, the light tower usually is placed near the end of the breakwater.

Cast-iron towers

Introduced as a building material in the 1840s, cast iron revolutionized lighthouse construction. Stronger than stone and relatively light, cast iron made it possible to fabricate the parts of a light tower in a far-off foundry and then ship them to the construction site for assembly.

Characteristic

The identifying feature of a lighthouse beacon. To help mariners tell one beacon from another, maritime officials gave each light a distinct color or pattern of flashes.

Clamshell or bivalve lenses

Most Fresnel lenses are round, but some have a slightly squeezed or flattened shape somewhat like that of a clamshell. They nearly always feature a pair of bull's-eyes or focal points, one on each side of the lens.

Clockwork mechanism

Early rotating lighthouse lenses were often driven by a set of gears, weights, and pulleys similar to those used in large clocks. Every few hours, the keeper had to "rewind" the machinery by pulling or cranking the weights to the top of the tower.

Coast Guard, United States

Since 1939, lighthouses and other aids to navigation in the United States have been the responsibility of the U.S. Coast Guard. Previously, the nation's maritime lights were maintained by a separate government agency known as the U.S. Lighthouse Service.

Elevation or height of the focal plane

Fresnel lenses and most modern optical systems channel light signals into a narrow band known as the focal plane. Because the curvature of the earth would render low-lying lights practically worthless for navigation, a coastal beacon must have an elevated focal plane. The height of the plane above the water's surface—usually from 40 to 200 feet—helps determine the range of the light.

Fixed signal

A lighthouse beacon that shines constantly during its regular hours of operation is said to display a "fixed" signal.

Flashing signal

A lighthouse beacon that turns on and off or grows much brighter at regular intervals is called a flashing signal.

Fog signal or foghorn

A distinct sound signal, usually a horn, trumpet, or siren, used to warn vessels away from prominent headlands or navigational obstacles during fog or other periods of low visibility.

Fresnel lenses

Invented in 1822 by Augustin-Jean Fresnel, a noted French physicist, Fresnel lenses concentrate light into a powerful beam that can be seen over great distances. Usually, they consist of individual hand-polished glass prisms arrayed in a bronze frame. Manufactured by a number of French and British companies, these devices came in as many as eleven different sizes, or orders. A massive first-order lens may be more than 6 feet in diameter and 12 feet tall, while a diminutive sixth-order lens is only about 1 foot wide and not much larger than an ordinary gallon jug.

Gallery

A circular walkway with a railing around the lantern of a lighthouse. Galleries provided keepers convenient access to the outside of the lantern for window cleaning, painting, and repair work.

Great Lakes lens

A type of lighthouse optic slightly smaller than a standard third-order Fresnel lens. Usually designated three-and-a-half-order lenses, they were among the largest optics in use on the Great Lakes.

Harbor light

A beacon intended to assist vessels moving in and out of a harbor. Not meant to serve as major coastal markers, harbor lights often consisted of little more than a lantern hung from a pole. However, many were official light stations, with a tower and residence for the keeper.

Keeper

Before the era of automation, responsibility for operating and main-taining a light station was placed in the hands of a keeper, sometimes aided by one or more assistants. During the eighteenth and nine-teenth centuries, keepers were appointed by the U.S. Treasury Department or even the president himself in return for military service or a political favor. Although the work was hard and the pay minimal, these appointments were coveted because they offered a steady income and free housing.

Keeper's residence or dwelling

The presence of a keeper's residence is what turned a light station into a light "house." Sometimes keepers lived in the tower itself, but a typical lighthouse dwelling was a detached one-and-a-half-story wood or stone structure built in a style similar to that of other working-class homes in the area.

Lamp and reflector

For several decades prior to the introduction of the highly efficient Fresnel lens, lighthouse beacons were intensified by means of lamp-and-reflector systems. These combined a bright-burning lamp and a polished mirror shaped in a manner intended to concentrate the light.

Lantern

The glass-enclosed space at the top of a light tower is known as the lantern. It houses the lens or optic and protects it from the weather.

Light tower

A tall, often cylindrical structure used to elevate a navigational light so that mariners can see it from a distance. Modern light towers support a lantern, which houses a lamp, electric beacon, or some other lighting device. Some light towers are an integral part of the station residence, but most are detached.

Lighthouse

A term applied to a wide variety of buildings constructed for the purpose of guiding ships. Often it is used interchangeably with similar or derivative terms such as *light tower* and *light station*. Throughout this book you will often find the more general term *light* used in reference to individual lighthouses or light stations.

Lighthouse Board

Beginning in 1851 and for more than half a century afterwards, U.S. lighthouses were administered by a Lighthouse Board consisting of nine members. Usually board members were noted engineers, scientists, and military men. Creation of the board brought a fresh professional spirit and penchant for innovation to the Lighthouse Service. Perhaps the board's most telling change was adoption of the advanced Fresnel lens as the standard U.S. lighthouse optic.

Lighthouse Service

A common term applied to the various organizations or agencies that built and maintained U.S. lighthouses from 1789 until 1939, when the U.S. Coast Guard was placed in charge.

Lighthouse tenders

The U.S. Lighthouse Service and later the U.S. Coast Guard maintained a small fleet of freighters and work vessels to help build and supply lighthouses. They were vital to remote lighthouse stations and offshore towers, which otherwise would have been impossible to provision. By tradition, many lighthouse tenders were given the names of flowers, such as *Marigold* and *Hyacinth*.

Lightships

Equipped with their own beacons, usually displayed from a tall central mast, lightships were essentially floating lighthouses. They marked shoals and key navigational turning points where construction of a permanent light tower was either impossible or prohibitively expensive.

Light station

A navigational facility with a light beacon is commonly referred to as a light station. Often the term is used interchangeably with *lighthouse*, but a light station may or may not include a tower, quarters for a keeper, and a fog signal.

Modern optic

A term referring to a broad array of lightweight, mostly weatherproof devices that produce the most modern navigational lights.

Occulting or eclipsing light

There are several ways to produce a beacon that appears to flash. One is to "occult" or block the light at regular intervals, often with a rotating opaque panel.

Private aid to navigation

A privately owned and maintained navigational light. Often, such lights are formerly deactivated beacons that have been reestablished for historic or aesthetic purposes.

Range lights

Displayed in pairs, range lights help mariners keep their vessels safely within the narrow navigable channels that crisscross estuaries or lead in and out of harbors. The rear-range light is higher and farther from the water than its partner, the front-range light, which is often located at water's edge. When viewed from mid-channel, the lights appear in perfect vertical alignment. If the upper light tilts either to the right or the left, a helmsman must steer in the opposite direction to correct course.

Skeleton towers

Iron- or steel-skeleton light towers consist of four or more heavily braced metal legs topped by workrooms and/or a lantern. Relatively durable and inexpensive, they were built in considerable numbers during the latter half of the nineteenth century. Because their open walls offer little resistance to wind and water, these towers proved ideal for offshore navigational stations, but some, such as the 145-year-old skeleton tower at Whitefish Point on the Michigan Upper Peninsula, were built on land.

Solar-powered optic

Nowadays, many remote lighthouse beacons are powered by batteries recharged during the day by solar panels.

Wickies

Before electric power made lighthouse work much cleaner and simpler, nearly all navigational beacons were produced by oil or kerosene lamps. Most of these lamps had wicks that required constant care and trimming. Consequently, lighthouse keepers often referred to themselves somewhat humorously as "wickies."

ABOUT THE AUTHORS

Photographs by **Bruce Roberts** have appeared in numerous magazines, including *Life* and *Sports Illustrated*, and in hundreds of books, many of them about lighthouses. He was director of photography at *Southern Living* magazine for many years. His work is also on display in the permanent collection at the Smithsonian Institution. He lives in Morehead City, North Carolina.

Ray Jones is the author or coauthor of fourteen best-selling books about lighthouses. He has served as an editor at Time-Life Books, as founding editor of *Albuquerque Living* magazine, as writing coach at *Southern Living* magazine, and as founding publisher of Country Roads Press. He lives in Pebble Beach, California, where he continues to write about lighthouses and serves as a consultant to businesses, publishers, and other authors.